I Decided

Kelly Holtman

Copyright © 2024 Kelly L. Holtman

All rights reserved.

ISBN: 979-8-218-37799-1

DEDICATION

I dedicate this book to my son, Nathan Holtman, whose character is unparalleled.

CONTENTS

Acknowledgments /i
Introduction / 1

1 Decide to Leap / 3

2 Knocking Is Required / 15

3 The Decisive Turn / 24

4 Persist or Surrender / 35

5 Protagonist of One / 40

6 Crafting Decisions Guided by Values / 47

7 My Decision / 50

8 Delaying the Blessing / 60

9 Unveiling the Art of Choice / 68

10 Making Effective Decisions / 78

11 Pray For Courage, Not a Rescue / 88

12 Practical Decision-Making Strategies / 94

13 The Power of Small Decisions / 100

ACKNOWLEDGMENTS

I am deeply grateful to my incredible son, Nathan for his unwavering support. His dedication in reading both my initial attempts and final draft has been invaluable. I am truly blessed to be his mom and I genuinely aspire to embody the qualities that make him so remarkable. I extend a heartfelt thank you to my sister, Shari, whose compliments of each draft gave me the courage to actually publish this book. Her encouragement across every facet of my life has served as a constant source of strength. To my countless friends, your warmth and kindness were the bedrock that sustained me through the toughest of days.

Lastly, my deepest appreciation extends to every person who has shared their story of transformation with me personally and also to those people who have shared their stories with the world in print or through other media. Because of you, I decided to write this book.

INTRODUCTION

I decided to write this book
You decided to read it.

Greatness begins with a simple phrase, "I Decided". Those two words are the declaration that signify a pivotal moment in one's life, marking a commitment to change. They precede the events that will probably be the worst and best of your life. When your desire to change your life outweighs your tolerance for the way it is, you will make a decision, and the change will begin. Deciding is different from wishing. Wishing is a hopeful desire without action. It does not require effort. Wishing can often be disguised as prayer followed by a long period of waiting, as waiting has become the virtue of the day. We hear phrases like "if it's meant to be, it will be". However, there will be no change

I DECIDED

until you decide there will be a change. Decideds require action. Yes, I just did that. I turned that adjective into a noun: DECIDEDS are the precursors to your blessings. Decideds fundamentally and forever change your life!

1 DECIDE TO LEAP

If this book has found its way into your life – by purchase, gift, or luck, then I believe you have a DECIDED waiting for you. Your Decided could be a simple dream that you've been contemplating, gradually transforming, and expanding your 'what if' from a fantasy to a burning desire. Alternatively, your Decided might require a major life overhaul born out of true misery or profound dissatisfaction. Either way, you understand that you must bid farewell to something or someone today and be prepared to risk losing it or them forever in order to pursue a more joyful tomorrow. Change always requires an exchange. It requires a sacrifice.

I am writing this book with a specific focus on decisions that are intended to bring positive changes in your life. However, I acknowledge that not all decisions are made with this goal in mind. While I do not fully comprehend why some people make decisions that inevitably and knowingly bring harm to themselves and others, I acknowledge the complexity of human behavior and the myriad factors that influence decision-making. My aim is to shed light on the power of intentional decisions for positive transformation, recognizing that the path to understanding the darker aspects of decision making may not be fully illuminated. Nonetheless, I hope to inspire and empower readers to make choices that lead to a more fulfilling and uplifting life journey. While my perspective in this book is rooted in my Christian beliefs and faith in God, I want to emphasize that the principles shared are universal and can be valuable to individuals from all walks of life, regardless of their religious or spiritual beliefs. The guidance provided is meant to be inclusive and supportive of diverse perspectives. In this book, you'll find references to prayer and God that are integral to my personal journey. It's important to note that your interpretation and connection with these concepts are entirely your own. Whether you find strength in prayer, meditation, or other sources, the aim is to provide a space for your personal reflection and growth, respecting your individual beliefs and experiences.

The concept of risk and reward is fundamentally about balance. The common belief is that the greater the risk, the greater the reward, but this is not always accurate. I have observed that some risks may seem small but can yield great rewards – especially over time - while other more significant risks ultimately provide no reward. In order to reduce uncertainty when taking risks in our businesses and personal lives, we shift our language from 'risk' to 'leap'. It's all about semantics! Leaving a job to pursue entrepreneurial endeavors is no longer a risk so much as it becomes a leap, suggesting courage and promise. A leap, as defined by Merriam-Webster means to spring free from, to act precipitately, to pass abruptly from one state to another. Therefore, taking a leap implies that the leaper is trying to suddenly move on purpose in order to create change. If we take a leap with no guarantee of success and no proof that our initial assumptions are correct, it's called a leap of faith. Faith is a word that implies trust and confidence.

Some individuals approach their life change, their leap, with great precision. They meticulously plan each step, mark each landing point, strategize the milestones, factor in contingencies, and work backward from their ultimate objectives keeping to a specific timeline. Others simply choose to wing it and hope for the best, improvising with no definite path to follow. Regardless of the approach, every leap is followed by a landing. At times the landing is swift, the goal is achieved, and the victory is apparent. However, what happens when your leap takes longer than expected? What if you land but find yourself off course or questioning your end goal? These are the questions that challenge us to reassess our goals and adapt to the unforeseen twists that life throws our way.

Many leaps can be taken without much disruption to your current life; however, this book focuses primarily on the leaps that inevitably disrupt our lives. These disruptions might include foregoing steady income in order to launch a business, pursuing a job in a new industry, saying "yes" to a marriage proposal, or initiating divorce proceedings. Your desired leap does not have to be grand like saving the manatees or leaving a legacy for generations to come. Your desire may be simply to bring joy into your own world. Saving the world, or the people and creatures in it, may be a byproduct of your leap, but for now, concentrate on improving your immediate circumstances by serving your community. A natural consequence to serving and offering value is that you are rewarded. History is often rewritten, and achievements are embellished or erased. Don't concern yourself with what may or may not be written about you.

I DECIDED

An example of an individual who leaps with precision would be someone who begins with a formal written business plan. Next they establish the business legally registering the business name, obtain a tax ID, obtain licenses and permits, and possibly open a bank account. Next they secure funding, hire team members, and find a suitable venue for offering their product or services. Once these tasks are complete, they presell orders, arrange for manufacturing, set appointments, or prepare presentations. In contrast, the leapers who prefer to wing it have no master plan, and no comprehensive task list to check off. Instead, they embark on a journey of mini leaps and small steps, allowing their endeavors to evolve organically until one day they unexpectedly find themselves with a fully functioning business. Only you will know which is the best path for you. Surprisingly, a well-crafted plan can still falter, while a plan lacking structure can flourish. In light of this, I contend, that a DECIDED mindset is the crucial component of achieving success. Whether you are a precision leaper or someone who embraces uncertainty, being decisive in your actions and resolute in your commitment can greatly impact the outcome of your endeavors. Throughout this book we will delve into the power of decisive choices and how they can shape the course of our lives, even amidst disruptive leaps, pandemics, naysayers, and critics.

In the space between taking a leap and achieving your dream lies a chasm of fear. If you have taken a leap and find yourself still aloft – or worse, falling - don't give up! Decide to keep going! Just as Pastor Joel Osteen says, you may just be closer than you think! There are countless stories of people on the verge of giving up who experience a glimmer of hope that ultimately becomes their turning point toward success. If you feel powerless and vulnerable in the midst of your leap, that doesn't mean that you made a wrong decision. It simply means that you are still in the process. It's okay to feel helpless, like a lost kitten, unsure of what to do next. It's also okay to surrender and seek mercy at your circumstances by asking for help or by admitting you feel weak in this moment. Your current vulnerability will allow you to build experience and thrive later on even though you may feel like you're barely surviving now. Every grown cat who defends itself with 'murder mittens' was once a purring kitten who had no option but to grow and learn through good decisions and bad. Typically, during moments of weakness we ask God for small miracles, with a prayer centered around survival, asking for simple yet impactful interventions, like securing a single sales order that would generate the revenue needed to cover this month's bills. I urge you to refrain from offering those small prayers.

I DECIDED

Instead of pleading with God for just enough to get by, start thanking Him for the abundance of resources, opportunities and ideas that are on their way to you. Thank Him for the blessings you've received throughout your life so far and pray bold prayers of faith full of expectation for overflow.

> "God won't help whimpering kitty cats. He helps Roaring Lions!"
> - Pastor Collin Higginbottom, Pathfinders Conference 2020.

Without ceasing, remind yourself why you were compelled to make a change in the first place and focus on the action that followed. As time goes by and you create more distance from your former situation it's easy to forget the pain and discomfort you were experiencing. We look back at our old life with fondness and longing but overlook the daily discomfort we experienced. We may even deduce that our dreams were better off simply as a fantasy we mentally indulged in and now we wonder why we were not content with what we had. Many people are too fearful to make a decision that will disrupt their lives. If you have indeed made such a decision, you demonstrate a rare and courageous spirit. I once made a decision in my career that disrupted my life, and despite knowing that it was the right thing to do, I still found myself doubtful and weeping as the reality of that decision set in. The fear and second-guessing that set in shortly after taking action on that decision shook me to the core. Nevertheless, I kept reminding myself of the reasons why I took the leap in the first place. I had the foresight to write document those reasons, my 'why', before making the leap. Reading my own words over and over again in the weeks that followed, eventually my tears dried up. It's perfectly fine to let the tears flow as you confront your fears. It's also important to realize that the first leap you take may not be the only one you will need to make. You may need to take a series of refined leaps in order to achieve your anticipated goal. Each new leap is born from a new decision based on more knowledge and experience gained through success and failure of the previous one. What may have looked like a failure was the very element necessary to get you to the next step.

I wrote this book not only for people who purposefully decide to change their world. I also wrote this book for those who are forced into change without a voice, having no contribution in the decision. A leap is supposed to be a purposeful action, but if you find yourself in the midst of a crisis, feeling this DECIDED was decided for you - you were laid off from your job, discarded by your spouse, diagnosed with an illness - I want you to know that you are not alone. Although it may seem like your circumstances are out of your control, you can still make purposeful decisions. In fact, you may be luckier than those who have had the luxury of choice. You have the gift of fewer regrets, not having to weigh the options of staying or leaving. Instead, you were pushed! Perhaps your behavior or actions caused you to be in that situation, and for that you might feel regret, but I suggest you discard the negative emotions quickly. There was a reason for your behavior and if you are truly honest with yourself you may realize that your soul was acting out in a fight for freedom. You can decide to see this situation you are faced with as a blessing or a curse. If you behaved poorly and are stubborn, are unwilling to make a change to your personality, or you choose to focus on the negative, then your pain will last longer. Nevertheless, this crisis may be the push you needed to finally make a change toward living the life you were meant to live. I believe that God is working in your favor, and you can decide right now that you are going to embrace this challenge and see it as a gift. I urge you not to dwell on what you can't change and trust that everything will work out for the best. You may or may not have behaved poorly in the past, but now is the time to forgive yourself, regardless, and focus on becoming a person you truly admire. Often the darkest moments lead you to the brightest future.

Some people are trapped in a cycle of misery where they actively cling to suffering, struggling with the dilemma of whether to remain where they are or to take the leap, as if gravity is holding them down. They justify their tolerance of the circumstances by comparing their situation to that of other people who are worse off, expressing gratitude merely for the lack of imagined tragedies. I was intimately acquainted with this comfort zone. Instead of seeking genuine blessings, my life consisted of continuous praises to God for sparing me from car accidents and food poisoning. Yet this is not the life that God wants for you or for anyone. Gratitude serves as a doorway to accepting that you are inherently worthy and deserving of good things, rather than merely expecting the absence of misfortune. This is your reminder that you possess the authority to define your own worth. In the realm of self-love, adorning your crown is a declaration that you are the ruler of your destiny, capable of leading your life with confidence, resilience, and grace.

> "I decided early on that I was going to put on my crown and rule my world by acting right and treating myself like a queen."
> - Queen Latifah

I DECIDED

From my personal observations, the majority of the people I know find contentment in their job, they collect their paycheck, and head home to a place they delight in. They enjoy their coworkers, lifestyle, and are content with their earnings. They fill their evenings and weekends with friends and activities that fulfill them. While some may aspire for more, the perceived effort and trade-offs involved in taking action to achieve greater goals are often considered not worth the hassle. Theirs is an enviable and admirable position, one marked with satisfaction and happiness. If you are in this place, please realize that my words are not meant to criticize your decision to stay where you are, nor are they meant to convince you that you want to change your circumstances. I too was content and happy for several decades before I began to desire more. There is a part of me that wishes I could have remained content. I earned a good living and had a worthwhile job, but I became restless and wanted more fulfillment, more financial security, and more freedom. Previous to that I was in a marriage that brought me happiness and laughter, until it no longer did. In each case, I sought a deeper sense of joy that I sensed was absent.

To me, being joyful differs from being happy. Joy is enduring and resilient, even in the face of disappointments, to the extent that your circumstances cannot plunge you into sadness. Tragedies touch everyone, and they can momentarily steal your joy, however being joyful means that you can appreciate the love and blessings surrounding you in the midst of the sorrow. I longed for that kind of enduring joy, and I believe you do too. I wrote this book out of love and a genuine desire to help you decide to be joyful.

> "You never become what you feel, but what you decide."
> – Rex Crane

2 KNOCKING IS REQUIRED

As mentioned in the previous chapter, some risks are monumental, such as leaving your job to start your own business, proceeding with a voluntary cosmetic procedure, or cutting ties with a long-time friend who delights in your misery. On the other hand, some decisions may seem simple and obvious, at least to someone who isn't making that decision. Take for instance weight management and a decision to shed weight. Notice that I chose that word 'shed' deliberately rather than the common word 'lose'. Lost things beg to be found and restored while things that are shed have been discarded for good. Be mindful of the words you choose each day.

I DECIDED

I won't discuss why a person's weight holds significance in our society, I merely use the analogy because shedding weight is a struggle that many individuals relate to. It may seem an impossible task, and if there are underlying medical reasons perhaps it is, but in general it is a common occurrence. Many of us have friends who've done it. We have coworkers and neighbors who boast about having done it. We even see photos of strangers on the internet sharing their before and after success photos. The weight 'loss' industry is enormous, encompassing various methods of weight loss including exercise routines, physical devices, and dietary plans. The decision to embark on a weight change journey may be simple, but the actual process is far from easy, and is often riddled with confusion. Growing up with a mother who was subjected to unsolicited comments about her skinny physique, I understand that weight-related issues are intricate and multifaceted. They are not isolated to individuals who weigh more than they desire to. All her life people thoughtlessly remarked to my mother "you're so skinny!" because, in fact, she was. She weighed approximately 85 pounds and on her 5'8" frame, that was very slim. Strangers would approach her with this declaration about her size, as if she wasn't aware of her own body. Such unsolicited focus on her appearance understandably left her feeling distressed, as it would anyone whose weight was thrust into focus.

For individuals who have never felt the need to either shed or gain weight, it might be challenging to comprehend the hesitation surrounding such a decision. However, for the person making the decision they realize this will require not only a change in their diet and exercise habits, but also a change in how they spend their time, how they spend their money, and how they interact with friends and family. So much of life is shared at the dinner table and many social settings often involve alcoholic beverages and light hors d'oeuvres . For many people these meaningful moments are a key aspect of their life, or quite possibly the only leisure human interaction they have, and they may worry that embarking on a weight altering journey will jeopardize these cherished connections. They may feel that the only way to control their intake is to avoid these functions altogether.

Furthermore, the focus of shedding weight might also shine a light on a person's alcohol consumption, potentially making them hesitant to address their weight-related concerns at all. While a person may desire weightshed (yes, I did it again - I made my own word), and may even make some progress, until they make a firm decision that they are going to shed the weight, success may elude them. There are exceptions of course, but I contend that if a person decides to shed or gain weight, fully accepts the lifestyle changes that are required, and diligently persists in the necessary actions, they will succeed. This is the power that deciding gives you. Decide to commit to the necessary actions and decide every day that you will not be swayed. I have known many people who desire to shed pounds and the ones who succeeded all included the words 'I decided' in some form or another as they describe to me their DECIDED moment with clarity and precision.

You do not have to justify your decision to anyone. Recommit each day and your decision will become more powerful than your cravings. You may find that prayer and meditation are useful tools. One final note on this point: you can decide to accept and love your body just as it is.

If you've attempted to change your life without success, then it is possible that your focus has been primarily on the desired outcome, without firmly committing to the necessary actions to bring about that change. Additionally, it's essential to consider that your decision must be unrealistic, in both time and scope. While you certainly have the power to decide to become an astronaut or world-famous basketball player, these aspirations come with prerequisites. If you lack the foundational requirements for these goals, no matter how resolute your decision and diligent your actions, achieving them might remain beyond reach. Moreover, you can decide to participate in this endeavor in a fashion that is more suited to your skills and abilities.

Nevertheless, your decisions must be backed up with persistent action even in the face of failures. In the words of Madame Leota in the film Haunted Mansion "You try, you fail, you try, you fail, but the only true failure is when you stop trying". This profound statement underscores the vital importance of perseverance once a decision has been made. She shared these words when character Jim Evers, played by Eddie Murphy when found himself locked outside of the mansion, desperately attempting to rescue his family trapped inside. Evers had given up on his rescue, but due to Madam Leota's words he made a resolute decision that he would enter the mansion, regardless of the obstacles. The instant he DECIDED, with absolute conviction that he would make it inside, he glimpsed the victory in his mind, and was therefore able to achieve it in real life. Well, in Hollywood real life anyway. Although this story is a work of fiction, its message resonates in real life.

Once you act on a decision, it becomes a permanent part of your personal history, much like the ringing of a bell that cannot be unrung. While you can certainly make a subsequent decision in an attempt to undo the first one, and any effects therefrom, that initial decision remains an indisputable part of your life's narrative. You can get back together with your girlfriend, but that does not undo the fact that you broke up with her in the first place. You can apologize for your harsh words, but even forgiveness will not erase them. Marriage is a decision with enduring consequences, even if annulments or divorces are sought and granted. The legal processes may dissolve a union, but they do not erase the initial commitment.

Likewise, tattoo removal, a costly and time-consuming procedure may erase the physical ink, however it cannot erase the fact that you made the decision to get the tattoo in the first place. Retrocausality remains an unproven concept in science; at least, it has not been substantiated thus far. Therefore, going back in time to undo past decisions is not within the realm of possibility. However, the reality of being unable to reverse past choices should not discourage you. Instead, it should serve as a source of empowerment, recognizing that you have the capability to make new decisions, or reaffirm your current ones each day.

Not every decision holds the power to reshape your entire life, but even those seemingly small choices can influence how you navigate and show up in your world. Regardless of the decision you are wrestling with, it's crucial to remember that you are worthy of the effort it takes to make it. You matter. Your life is significant. You are so valuable that God sent his only son so that you might live a joyful and prosperous life. You weren't designed to endure constant hardship and suffering and misery is not your default fate. You possess both the ability and the responsibility to make decisions that align with the desires of your heart, steering you closer to the life you want to lead. As you take small steps, you'll come to realize that you don't have to tread this path alone. Seeking help from others is not only important but sometimes necessary. Once you move, God moves with you. Even if you don't believe in a supreme being, you will see that once you take a step, the next step aligns in your favor.

> "Once you make a decision, the universe conspires to make it happen."
> – Ralph Waldo Emerson

I believe that prayers are often answered through action. It's as if God is saying "You make the first move, and we can get started". Instead of pleading for a rescue, express gratitude for the conviction of your decision and take actions toward achieving the outcome. You may have heard the saying "ask and you shall receive". I can already hear your response – you've asked, but you haven't received exactly what you asked for, within the time frame you desired, or in the manner you expected. If you find yourself wondering why your desires haven't materialized while you passively wait, it's likely because you may not yet be prepared for the change you seek. When you are truly ready, you will be compelled to take action.

Matthew 7 in the Bible says, "Ask, and it shall be given you; seek, and ye shall find; knock, and it shall be opened unto you". (KJV) In my interpretation (though you are welcome to have your own), this passage implies that action is required in order to receive. Start by asking for what you want, articulating your desires with precision and clarity, and then write them down. Asking for what you want is the initial step in creating a vision for your future. If you never voice your desires, they will forever remain mere wishes.

The next step is to seek a way to make it happen. Seek the knowledge, resources, tools, individuals, education, or anything else necessary to accomplish that desire. Seek guidance, seek funding, seek remedies, seek processes, seek clarity. Seek evidence of the goal achieved by looking to people who have achieved what you desire.

Lastly, take action by knocking on doors to create opportunities. Consider this: have you ever arrived at a friend's house, parked your car, and then waited on their doorstep, hoping they might have seen you arrive and would come open the door? How long would you linger there without knocking? If you stand at the door praying for your friend to open it, but you never actually make the effort to knock, then it's unfair to feel upset if your friend never opens the door. What if you arrive at a stranger's house who isn't even expecting you? If they do happen to see you lingering on their porch without knocking, they might call authorities for your removal assuming you are lost, confused or up to no good. To be acknowledged, you must announce your presence. You must take that vital step of action. You must knock.

> "You have to decide what you want to believe, and then you gotta do the really hard work to push yourself to take the action before you're ready."
>
> - Mel Robbins

> "The long-term impact of making a decision from your heart and soul, that is where the best life comes from, because you are living for what is true for you."
>
> - Mel Robbins

3 THE DECISIVE TURN

Although I have focused so far on major life changes, I want to emphasize that even seemingly small changes can have a significant impact. Again, simple is not synonymous with easy. Making a decision to change any part of your life takes courage, and I applaud your bravery in doing so. It's important to remember that small changes can have a ripple effect, but these ripples may not be symmetrical, flowing evenly from the epicenter outward. Sometimes, they may flow in one direction, perhaps one that aligns with the path you want for your life, or perhaps in a direction you don't desire. Your Decided will be a culmination of those small ripples. You may not even realize it at the time, but each decided builds on the last and propels you towards your ultimate goals, or away from them. The key is to make decisions that align with the direction you wish to move.

If you have reached the point where you know that a change is necessary, but you are struggling to make the decision to leap, please know that you are not alone. I have tremendous empathy for you. The prospect of leaping into the unknown can be profoundly daunting and overwhelming, especially when the path ahead appears unclear. However, living indefinitely in a state of indecision and longing can be just as formidable a challenge. I often wonder how many exceptional ideas will never be shared with the world out of fear and how many potential businesses will never be launched. It's disheartening to consider how many individuals will quit before crossing the finish line, paralyzed by their fears, or worse yet, how many will never even start. How long have you been living with indecision? And how much longer will you allow this indecision to persist?

It's entirely possible to indefinitely postpone making a decision. Some people continue living week after week, month after month, year after year, fully aware that they will, one day, make a decision to change their life. Internally they are hoping that some outside force changes it for them, so they don't have to take responsibility. Sadly, they persist in clinging to their jobs, their social circles, and their daily routines. Perhaps you can relate to this, harboring a desire for change but suppressing it, waiting for a more opportune moment. However, the longer you delay your decision, the longer your blessings are delayed. In the battle between faith and fear, faith can prevail, but only if you're willing to root your faith in action. Procrastinating when it comes to making a decision will take its toll on you, negatively affecting your mental, physical, and spiritual well-being. Traditional Chinese medicine, (TCM Theory) highlights the intimate connection between emotions and physical health. Each emotion is believed to be intricately linked to a corresponding organ of the body, impacting it either positively or negatively. The detailed intricacies of TCM Theory extend beyond the scope of this book, but I encourage you to research it further.

> "Something happened after I watched [The Secret] that was catalytic. I made the decision from that day on that I was going to put faith in what I believed."
> - David Metzler

If you're currently wrestling with feelings of anger, sadness, or confusion, I firmly believe it's a sign that you have a decision to make. Perhaps you've been avoiding it, fearing potential regret from the outcomes of your decision. Regret often finds its roots in fear. But don't worry about regretting your decision because you most likely will. At least at first, because every decision comes with a cost, akin to what is called "opportunity cost" in the financial world. Technically it refers to the potential gains foregone from other alternatives when one choice is made. In this context, the opportunity cost means making one decision precludes you from making another potentially more beneficial one. Your cost may be tangible like money, or it could be your time, or perhaps the loss of a person you care about who turns away from you because of your decision. Alternatively, it might be an intangible cost such as feelings of shame.

> "The heaviest things in life aren't iron and gold, but unmade decisions. The reason people feel stressed is because they have decisions to make but are not making them."
> – Alex Hormozi

Regardless, it's imperative to understand that with any decision, regardless of its scale, there exists a risk of regret, even if the outcome is favorable. Another truth worth noting is that even if you make the right decision, it doesn't necessarily translate to an overnight success. More than likely your progress will feature moments of success and failure and may take longer than you anticipate. Don't be fooled by the seemingly overnight success of some people. The truth is that you are only seeing the end result of years of struggle.

Following the initial high of making your decision and the exhilaration that comes with it, you'll eventually settle into a routine, which may be monotonous and possibly uncomfortable. Perhaps it involves cold calling, exercising, or saving money. At least these tasks are obvious action steps. Personally, I find that refraining from certain actions, embracing non-action steps, poses a more formidable challenge. I would much prefer to complete 20 sit-ups every hour than fast for a day.

Here's another undeniable truth, albeit a challenging one: you might actually fail. People fail all the time despite their well-laid plans, their unwavering persistence, the effort they invest and despite their decision to succeed. The key to overcoming the failure is to readdress your decision, figure out what went wrong, regroup, and try again. To overcome regret, you must cultivate a resolute determination to succeed. If you decide to succeed and keep trusting in your future self, then fruit will follow. Just be sure that you are planting your seeds in fertile soil. Decide to keep striving for the person who was brave enough to make the decision to leap in the first place. One effective way to tilt the odds in favor of success is to fix your gaze on your ultimate goal rather than dwelling on the failures and mistakes. Living in the past stirs anxiety and can cause you to second guess your decision, which can undermine the progress you've achieved.

I recently delved into Lindsey Vonn's book "Strong is the New Beautiful". Vonn is an Olympic skier, and her book explores the concept of harnessing your power through eating clean and disciplined living. A section of the book recounts how she was injured at the 2006 Olympic games in Italy and had to be air lifted off the mountain. In that moment she feared that she would never ski again. It looked like failure. Fortunately for her, nothing was broken nor beyond healing and she was able to finish the games. Several years later, two weeks before the 2010 Olympic games in Vancouver she crashed in a training session and had to be assisted off the mountain. This time she was forced to take a break from skiing in the weeks leading up to the games. She inevitably had to rethink her practice plans and focus on healing. She chose not to attend the opening ceremonies, instead using the crucial time to recover in her room. "It was a difficult decision to make", but one that she made in furtherance of her goal. Days later, after a delay due to weather, despite having a torn shin and bruised skin she was able to complete the race and win a gold medal. Days later she went on to win a bronze medal. Vonn's example features several key elements of a DECIDED, and those are maintaining flexibility with your action steps and unwavering determination.

I recommend creating a checklist outlining the action steps you're currently aware of that are required to work toward your goal. As you take action, new steps may emerge, so be sure to update the list accordingly and mark off the actions steps as you accomplish them. Include a section for noteworthy accomplishments that were not initially planned, but completed, nonetheless. This visual representation serves to motivate and provide clarity by highlighting your progress. If you encounter a juncture on your checklist where progress is no longer feasible, it becomes evident that a decision to either stop or pivot is needed. Making a decision, informed by the insights gained, or choosing to stop the project altogether is a valid and strategic move, especially if the passion for your project has waned, and your satisfaction came from the pursuit itself. The key lies in discerning whether your goal remains worthy and in alignment with your values. If your initial objective has evolved or circumstances have changed, adapting your path, or redirecting your efforts can be a prudent decision. The distinction between quitting and making a thoughtful shift is crucial, ensuring that your journey remains purposeful and in pursuit of a meaningful goal. Sometimes if your resources are exhausted, you may have no choice but to postpone or abandon your goal. Acknowledge the success you did achieve and be grateful as gratitude is the precursor to blessings.

Consider this, for instance: if you decide to open an Italian restaurant and invest three years of your life into it, only to eventually close it, you have indeed succeeded. You succeeded in conceptualizing, opening, operating, and eventually closing the restaurant. The fact that the endeavor didn't unfold exactly as you expected for as long as you hoped, does not equate to failure. Even a single day of service, a single customer, or a single well-prepared dish can be counted as a success.

However, if you are plagued by regret over past decisions, it may indicate you're still closely connected to your former self, the one who had not yet summoned the bravery to leap. What small step can you take right now that will ripple into your future. Regret can never completely be avoided as it is an inevitable part of life. It's a choice between regretting your decision and actions you took or regretting not making a decision at all. The clearest path to overcoming regret is to succeed, but if success is not achieved then you can at least be proud of your motives. If your objective is ethical and praiseworthy, then take solace in the knowledge that you made an effort. However, if your actions are bound to inflict harm, it's imperative to thoughtfully evaluate your motives. Reflect on the ethical implications and moral considerations associated with your goal. Sometimes, a deeper examination of motives may reveal alternative paths that align with your objectives without causing harm to others. Taking the time for this thoughtful evaluation ensures that your pursuit is not only personally fulfilling but also ethically sound and considerate of the well-being of those who might be affected.

Victory is apparent when you gain something you were seeking: the million-dollar business, the featured art show, or the gold medal. But goals do not always involve gaining or achieving something tangible. Goals and desires that promise a tangible reward for their achievement often feel more straightforward to pursue compared to those that seem to offer no immediate return. Perhaps the change you seek in your life is to eliminate something or break a habit. Setting a clear goal, such as climbing Mount Everest may include obvious action steps that are explicit and clear: choose the dates, buy a permit, book the flight, hire the guides, buy the equipment, train for a year, plan the route, and then you go. It's relatively straightforward to mark each of these tasks off your checklist because embedded within each of these actions is a tiny "Decided".

However, defining success in the context of breaking a habit can be nuanced. How do you measure success in and endeavor that must be measured daily for the rest of your life? For instance, if your goal is to attain sobriety for the two weeks that your parents will be visiting, and you were able to that, then you achieved success. If your goal however is lifelong sobriety, when do you acknowledge success? There is no agreed upon timeframe that marks sobriety. In my twenties, a friend confided in me that he was an alcoholic and asked me to accompany him to an AA meeting. While at the meeting, I heard a man describe himself as a 'recovering alcoholic', having been sober for over 30 years. What struck me was that he still labelled himself as a 'recovering alcoholic'. I believe that words carry significance and can influence us. While counting the days, months or years since your last drink can serve as motivation, and obviously recognizes a remarkable achievement, it should be utilized as a tool rather than an absolute authority. A person's identity does not belong to a habit they once had. Although keeping track is valuable, and necessary for some individuals, I hope those with this DECIDED embrace their new identity as a sober person as quickly as possible and move beyond their history. The benchmark of your life is not defined by the number of alcohol-free days; you can decide on a predetermined date to stop counting and cease anchoring your identity to that last drink. Temptation may persist, but temptation is not defeat.

> "I decided to stop drinking while it was still my idea."
> - Billy Connolly

> "Since the day I decided to become sober and a mother, I've been trying to become who I am supposed to be."
> - Glennon Doyle Melton

4 PERSIST OR SURRENDER

Once you've firmly made a decision, it's important to recognize that there is no going back. That may sound contradictory to what I wrote in the previous chapter. What I mean is that while you can take a break, hit pause, pivot, or even quit, the decision itself remains irreversible. There is no returning to the life you had before taking the leap. Making a decision means declaring war on the situation that you have been enduring. It is a commitment to change signifying that your situation has become too painful, monotonous, or unfulfilling to bear any longer. If fear or the belief of failure starts to surface, there might be temptation to backtrack and undo your decision. However, even if you succumb to this temptation, your life will never fully revert back to what it once was. The decision itself becomes an unforgettable chapter of your personal history.

Some individuals find relief by giving up, cherishing a deeper appreciation for their former life. Activities that were once a source of annoyance are now approached with a newfound delight. Conversely, for others, the experience of surrendering their dream is more painful, yet they take solace in the knowledge that they gave it their best effort. Regardless of their emotions, the attempt satisfies their curiosity about what could have been and puts to rest the endless 'what-ifs'. The mental exploration of the what-ifs often proves more agonizing than the tangible negative outcome. Curiosity kindles desire and once that curiosity is satisfied, the desire can be set aside. Nevertheless, life undergoes a permanent shift because the dream is no longer undecided. The question mark has transformed into a period.

If you know that returning to your old life will deplete your soul, then I urge you to persevere and not give up! A more fulfilling life awaits you, and it's essential for you to discover a path forward. While you don't necessarily need a grand purpose in life, having a sense of purpose is crucial because it will keep you motivated during the tough times.

I recommend praying for inspiration, seeking ideas, asking for support from loved ones, and even strangers. Allow your imagination to guide you toward your purpose recalling Einstein's wisdom: "Imagination is everything. It is the preview of life's coming attractions." If you can imagine it, you can achieve it with the right resources. Granted, unlimited resources such as money, time, and connections, would nearly ensure success, but such abundance is rare. Typically, people don't abandon their dreams due to lack of faith or imagination; it's more often because they've run out of resources. Thus, success requires mindful management of your available resources.

Making the decision to terminate a relationship with someone you deeply care about whether it's a romantic partner, family member, or long-time friend, can be one of the most agonizing choices you face. Yet, keeping someone in your life who causes you pain, whether intentionally or not, is profoundly detrimental to your spirit and destructive to your body. The emotions of sadness, longing and neglect can be overwhelming. Sadness is a form of pain. Longing is a form of pain. Neglect is a form of pain. It's crucial to approach this decision judiciously and seek the counsel of a professional or trusted confidant before you finalize your decision. However, once the decision is made, there is no going back to the way things were, even if no action is taken. The decision becomes etched in your mind, complicating all subsequent thoughts on the matter. Once you take action, the same principle applies – it is irreversible, even if you wish otherwise. Taking deliberate steps to create distance from someone means that any attempt at reconciliation, whether in thought or in reality, might result in perceived improvements, but the relationship can never fully revert to its original state prior to the distancing action. This change will be fundamental, either in a positive direction, or a negative one.

Regardless of the source of your pain, once you have made the decision to leap, persisting in the same way of life becomes intolerable. Each time you are confronted with the unbearable situation, your reaction intensifies. Feelings of longing or boredom will become more pronounced, prompting you to question if this is the extent of what life has to offer. People and images will highlight your discontent with the situation. As you lay sleepless at night, you'll reflect on how another day has passed without making any headway in altering your circumstances. You might attempt to rationalize and justify this pain by citing current responsibilities that cannot be set aside or placing blame on someone else for your present situation. Perhaps there is validity in your perspective. However, I assure you that there is something you can do today to improve your circumstances. Begin by cultivating gratitude for the blessings you already have and focus on what is working well in your life. Take a daily inventory of each positive occurrence and acknowledge that your destiny can change in an instant, through a single decision.

> "I'm going to be done when I've decided that I'm done."
> – David Ortiz

5 PROTAGONIST OF ONE

Your life is not a movie - well, not yet. The future remains uncertain, and its mysteries are yet to be unveiled. There's a chance that one day, a reader of this book might achieve fame and inspire a movie about their journey. If such a day happens, remember to send a shout-out my way!

It's important to remember that movies often romanticize the pursuit of our dreams. We're presented with a montage of sleepless nights and early mornings, a workspace cluttered with sticky notes and crumpled papers, alongside empty takeout boxes. Our protagonist, with her hair in a messy bun and a pencil tucked behind her ear, tirelessly types away at her laptop, clad in the same clothes she wore yesterday. We observe her at a coffee shop or on a park bench, occasionally pausing to glance at the passersby. Alternatively, she might be running up bleachers in the rain, seeking solace and clarity of mind. Then later, approaching the breakthrough, our protagonist, perhaps an artist, paints with a frenetic energy, blending Indigo Blue and New Gamboge in a smear of green on the canvas, moving around like a ninja amidst half-finished masterpieces. If this narrative takes the form of a love story, we, of course, are privileged to watch the protagonist pack her ex-lover's belongings into a tiny suitcase, tears glistening as she lingers over the cat figurine he gave her in remembrance of her deceased pet Luna. Most notably in this montage, we witness our hero repeatedly declining invitations from concerned friends, deliberately leaving text messages unread, relying on isolation as the means to resolve her challenges.

In reality, the individual diligently typing away at the keyboard has been immersed in the task for hours, not breezing through seconds in a cinematic montage. She feels tired, sore, dehydrated, and bored of Chinese food. The woman running bleachers is dealing with toe blisters and mental chatter that refuses to be outrun, no matter how long she strains her body. Reality is vastly different from the idealized scenes portrayed in movies. The mundane and repetitive actions that move us toward our dreams often don't feel like progress. They feel like stagnation or running on a hamster wheel. The intense focus and determination depicted in movies can, in real life, translate to moments of doubt and setbacks. The point is that you don't need to approach it like a movie montage. The accumulation of small steps can carry you a considerable distance. Just keep moving forward, and perhaps a bit sideways.

> "The hardest part when I decided to move into acting was trusting I'd made the right decision."
> – Caitriona Balfe

The belief that hard work and perseverance inevitably lead to rewards is ingrained in us, yet that does not prohibit doubt and fear from sneaking in. Probably because our logical mind recognizes that some rewards are just too far from reach. Furthermore, fatigue and overwhelm can make it difficult to prioritize ourselves and our goals, especially when we feel guilty for doing so. Our own thoughts can derail us at every turn. We might achieve small victories, such as acquiring a new client, setting a personal record on a run, or enjoying a date with someone special. However, after weeks or months, progress may seem stagnant allowing that doubt to creep back in, making it harder to push forward. In such moments, anchoring yourself in your Decided is crucial!

Despite meticulously following every guideline, and taking the right actions day after day, you may not see progress or any sign of change. Despite weeks of dedicated effort towards your goal, the desired reward seems elusive leading to considerable frustration. Especially when you've made the difficult cold calls, attended various networking events, worked diligently at enhancing your physique, saved your money and showed up for important events. The sought-after reward may appear to slip further away with each passing week. The harsh truth is that despite your unwavering effort, success may not materialize in the end. This realization can be devastating, leaving you feeling defeated and broken, sobbing from inexpressible pain. However, it's uncommon for any journey to be effortless ending with unimpeded success. Any every journey yields rewards if you are willing to look for them.

In real life, once you decide to leap, you're off-script; there's no rain to mask your tears or background music to accompany the sorrow. Unlike movies where the hero's struggles begin and end with credits marking a clear beginning and clear ending, our struggles persist throughout our lifetime – some big, some small. The unpredictability of our world contributes to our struggles, yet the beauty is that fate often brings what we need in life, not necessarily what we thought we wanted. Embrace the gift of unforeseen blessings that can enrich your life. Stay focused on your goals and remain open to unexpected sources of joy. Just as in movie making, you may exceed your budget, take longer to finish the project or experience rewrites mid-film, trust that your decision will be the right one.

> "There is no right decision in life, because every decision we make is new and unpredictable".
> – M.F. Moonzajer

Did you know that tears come in three types? First are the basal tears, which lubricate your eyes throughout the day. Second are the reflex tears, which clear irritants from the eyes. And the third type are emotional tears, arising in response to intense feelings like sadness, anger, or joy. In my opinion, the emotional tears serve as a way for our bodies to purge negative thoughts and emotions, rinsing away outdated beliefs and identities, preparing us for the person we will become. The falsehoods that maintained your façade that everything is fine are being exposed and discarded with the emotional tears. Dwelling on negative thoughts or past hurts extends the tears because you continually revisit your areas of pain, and mentally recreate the scenes that caused them. In these humbling moments, unable to stop the tears from flowing some people make bargains with God, others with the devil. If you have never prayed from a feeling of profound and utter despair, then you cannot fathom the pain that some people endure. I propose that you allow your body to cleanse itself by experiencing the tears fully and freely instead of fighting them. Purge the pain and leave the past behind you. Revisiting your past decisions or questioning your choices does not serve you. You cannot ever know if a different decision would have led to a more favorable outcome. You will never know. Trust God with your sorrow and remember to trust that the sorrow did not come to stay.

Another interesting theory I came across recently involves weight loss, to coin an old phrase. According to the theory, when fat cells are released, the emotions that accumulated during the development of those fat cells are also released. As a result, the individual may experience emotions such as happiness or shame, or any sentiment that was prevalent at the time when the fact cell originated.

According to ShapeReClaimed.com "It's the beginning of an emotional detox." My personal interpretation is that fat cells hold memories. If your goal is to improve your health or your appearance you might encounter challenges stemming from unexpected thoughts that seem to come from nowhere. It's plausible that resistance or lack of motivation serves as a defense mechanism against the release of suppressed emotions you don't want to confront. Your decision to change your body may be in alignment with or in opposition to these emotions. Understanding this concept may help you push through these difficult times.

> "Weight loss doesn't begin in the gym with a dumbbell: it starts in your head with a decision."
>
> – Toni Sorenson

6 CRAFTING DECISIONS GUIDED BY VALUES

We often use the phrase 'taking a leap' to describe pursuing our desires, implying it's as manageable as leaping over a tiny rain puddle. In reality, it's more akin to attempting to leap over the entire ocean. The challenge can seem overwhelming, characterized by periods of calm that extend for days, only to be disrupted like the turbulent North Sea waves in winter. Feeling scared before taking a leap is normal, and it's healthy to embrace the fear while also cultivating excitement about the potential future. In the final chapters of this book, I will offer recommendations to assist you in getting started. However, the most crucial advice I can offer is this: make a decision.

While in the midst of writing this book, a widely publicized incident occurred that captured global attention. It was the "slap heard around the world" in which Will Smith slapped Chris Rock at the Oscars in 2022. I had already incorporated the following quote by Smith in this chapter, and it prompted me to reconsider whether it should remain. However, I believe its relevance has only intensified. I initially came across this quote in a YouTube video titled 'Focus on Yourself Not Others', shared by the Law of Attraction Coaching channel on May 12, 2020:

> "You just decide, what it's going to be, who you're going to be, how you're going to do it, just decide. And then from that point the universe is going to get out of your way."
> - Will Smith

Smith is correct in that first you must decide. It's essential to start your journey with a clear decision, even if you don't have the clearest vision of the obstacles you may encounter. I initially included this quote because it emphasizes the importance of deciding to take action. However, it also illustrates that it's equally crucial to decide ahead of time what action not to take. Hasty decisions can lead to unfavorable outcomes, potentially damaging your reputation, could lead to legal consequences, financial ruin, or worse. Predicting unforeseeable events is impossible. In situations where your emotions are intensified and your instinct is to take immediate action, how do you approach decision-making? The truth is that you're more likely to react than make a decision. But you can make decisions ahead of time about your values and your behavior. By doing so you equip yourself with a guiding compass, enabling you to navigate life with clarity and purpose. It's a commitment to conscious living, enabling you to respond thoughtfully rather than react impulsively when faced with unpredictable or objectionable circumstances.

> "Deciding what not to do is as important as deciding what to do."
> - Steve Jobs

7 MY DECISION

The debate surrounding the choice between following one's passion and pursuing what one is skilled at remains an ongoing and unresolvable discussion. In my personal history, passions were often relegated to hobby status, separate from primary pursuits. As I write this book I am working in the financial services industry, having done so for nearly twenty years. However, I am also a visual artist who began painting almost thirty years ago. Painting holds a special place in my heart and is a calling I'm compelled to answer. Over the years, I have sold thousands of paintings both privately and through galleries, have won awards, and have served on several art boards. However, I realized early in my art career that I cherish parts of the process and loathe others. I greatly enjoy the creative process and the community, but I do not enjoy packaging and transporting paintings, nor do I enjoy the submission process for certain events.

Engaging with people at gallery shows is a cherished experience and I am continually amazed at the diverse audience interpretations of my work. Art has a way of eliciting personal memories, desires, and fears, serving as a canvas upon which people can project their own memories and motives. During gallery interactions, I am fascinated as viewers articulate the emotions my paintings evoke in them interpreting each piece like an inkblot in a therapy office – regardless of the actual image. The depth of their perception as they explore my paintings never fails to astound me. They noticed aspects that I overlooked because they bring their own history, prejudices, and biases to the piece. Their interpretations, in turn, alter my own perspective of my work in a captivating revelation.

Regrettably, there was a time when the act of painting felt more like a job than a passion. Commitments for shows, gallery displays, and especially commissioned sales turned the creative process into a labored production. I found myself avoiding painting altogether, opting instead to rearrange my pantry and organize my closet. My creativity felt stifled. Several of my friends earn their livelihood from selling their paintings but concern over losing my creativity and the overwhelming emphasis on creating solely for commercial purposes drained much of the joy from the experience. I found myself painting subjects that were popular and easily marketable, rather than indulging my creative impulses. I inadvertently fell into a cycle of monotony, and the love I once felt for each brushstroke began to wane.

Approximately ten years after I began painting I got divorced and for nearly fifteen years after that I set down my paintbrush. The responsibilities of raising my son and starting a new career consumed my time and energy, leaving little room for artistic pursuits. I am grateful for the years I spent married and for the ability to be a stay-at-home mom for ten years. I will cherish those years forever. However, post-divorce, I entered the workforce and during this phase of my life, I found contentment, satisfaction, and financial stability from my job. A serious of serendipitous events led me to apply for a position as a junior financial advisor. I was eager to pursue this role as I knew that I had untapped potential within me. I also had a personal history that compelled me to desire to work in this industry.

I accepted this opportunity; however, I was placed in a

support role that was intended to be temporary. That temporary position lasted approximately eight years. As each year passed I felt like the initial opportunity was slipping away. Throughout this time, my son grew up, went to college, and moved out. I found myself drawn back to painting and I realized that I liked living in two worlds: the analytical world of finance, and the creative world of art. This balance provided the soulful satisfaction I craved. There was no pressure to create art for the purpose of selling or showcasing in galleries. This time I painted for myself. I decided to allow my imagination to wander and explore subjects that captivated my thoughts - rabbit holes, seahorses, jungle temples - much like when I first started my artistic journey. While many of these paintings found buyers, the absence of the pressure to set up a show or attend gallery openings brought a sense of freedom. By letting go of the pursuit of art as a career, I rediscovered my love for it.

With my son in college, I found myself with an abundance of free time and I entered a new phase of life: dating. This marked a significant change for me after being single for nearly 15 years. Initially, the excitement of this new chapter provided a sense of adventure. However, deep down I wasn't sure what I was truly seeking and grappled with whether I wanted to pursue marriage or if I wanted to follow in the footsteps of Blanche Devereaux from Golden Girls. My indecision led to confusion and uncertainty that caused me to question my current life situation as a whole.

In 2019, while on a first date in a coffee shop, my date introduced me to podcasts. He demonstrated how to access various podcasts on my phone, and we listened to snippets of several. Later that week I stumbled upon a podcast by Cathy Heller, titled "Don't Keep Your Day Job". The podcast caught my attention because my job wasn't exactly fulfilling, and the podcast focused on turning your passion into a profit. Each day, I eagerly sought out another of Cathy's podcasts and found myself captivated by her guests and their compelling stories. Each and every guest shared their DECIDED moment – that pivotal point when they consciously chose to change their lives. The phrases "I decided" or "I made a decision" echoed repeatedly, underlining the profound impact of making a decision.

For instance, guest, Jennifer Weiner, a bestselling author, shared a personal anecdote about being dumped when she was 28. In the aftermath of heartbreak, she took stock of her coping tactics, identifying storytelling as a powerful tool. She recalls, "I decided I'm going to tell myself a story where the girl is like me, the guy is like him, and the girl is going to have a happy ending." S3 E60. Those words propelled her to a new level in her career.

I DECIDED

Adding to my admiration of this podcast series was Cathy's genuine voice and the sincere manner in which she connected to her guests and audience. I felt as though she was speaking directly to me. I visited the library in my neighborhood and borrowed Cathy's book eager to delve into her story, anticipating it held answers to questions I hadn't even realized I was seeking.

In her book, Cathy vividly recounts her childhood, the enduring sadness, and the eventual rejection from the people closest to her. Her story resonated with me so deeply that I was mentally transported back to my own childhood. My parents never rejected me, however I often felt overlooked. They were preoccupied with their own struggles and tragedies, leaving my siblings and I to fend for ourselves. I recall a third-grade teacher presiding over the lunchroom when she noticed that I rarely had lunch and on the occasions when I did bring lunch it usually consisted of a small baggie of dry cereal and nothing more. When confronted, I admitted to packing my own lunch every day and soon after that, I began working in the cafeteria to earn my 'free' lunch. Years later, during college, I asked my mom about this situation, and she confessed that it never occurred to her or my dad to make me lunch because I had never asked them to. I hold no ill will toward my parents, as they worked tirelessly to simply survive, but it never occurred to me that should have asked for the bare minimum.

The truth was, I rarely sought help from my parents because the usual response was something along the lines of 'you're so smart, I'm sure you'll figure it out on your own', or 'you've got this'. It was, in fact, a polite "no". While some people recount experiences of parents belittling them or making them feel inadequate, my parents took the opposite approach. They frequently praised my intelligence, independence and expressed pride in my abilities. This fostered a belief in me that I needed to handle everything on my own, flawlessly. By the time I entered college, I had internalized the notion that asking for help was pointless, leading me to adopt a perpetual do-it-alone mindset that persisted well into my adulthood. While I often encounter the polite 'no' with the familiar "you can do it", there is one realm where I consistently find help whenever I seek it – through prayer with God.

When Heller was 25 years old, she had a lucrative job that provided for all of her material needs. On the surface, she seemed to have it all. Despite this, she grappled with a deep sense of imposter syndrome, feeling that she was not living up to her true potential. It became increasingly evident that her job and her actions were out of sync with her heart's desires. Eventually, the undeniable truth of this misalignment hit her. She recounts, 'I was sobbing on the side of the interstate when I decided, I can't do this anymore'. There it was again – those two words: "I DECIDED". Despite her discontent, her life had remained in a state of inertia until that pivotal day - the day she decided to change it.

Heller's book and podcasts inspired a spirit in me as I realized that I no longer wanted to work at a job that left me unfulfilled, with only scant hours of happiness during evenings and weekends. My purpose was no longer simply to work to pay bills for myself and my son as it had been for so many years. I aspired to craft a life that I genuinely enjoyed living. Despite this realization, I struggled to envision what that life would entail.

Soon, a truly remarkable occurrence unfolded in my personal life. I began to hear the phrase "I Decided" in stories of ordinary people all around me every day. The words were spoken in stories of people leaving toxic relationships, transforming fitness habits, changing career paths, and pursuing life-long dreams. The prevalence of those words was astounding! It led me to a profound realization: I felt I had uncovered the key differentiator between those who achieve their goals and those who do not. It all boiled down to one simple truth – they decided.

I had no idea how I would achieve the life I desired; I couldn't even clearly envision what that life looked like. However, I made a firm decision to do whatever it took to pursue the freedom my soul yearned for. Cathy Heller's podcast played a transformative role for me. The insightful discussions and courageous guests inspired me to explore my own passions and purpose. Although the change wasn't immediate, as fear and a desire for comfort initially held me back, little did I know then that my decision to pursue change would eventually cost me my job, my security, and my peace.

One day I decided it was time to stop playing it safe and I mustered the courage to ask for the promised opportunity to become a financial advisor. My boss granted me the title; however, I was expected to continue in my current support role as well. This was fair since I was still receiving my full salary for that role, however I found myself at a crossroads, unsure of how to effectively transition from my old responsibilities to fully embrace this new position. I managed to secure a few clients, but because I was unable to fully shed my previous role I was unable to envision myself as an advisor. I also lacked the confidence to allow others to envision me that way. My life continued much as it had been, with little change and no progress. Life maintained its predictable and mundane course. I suspect this experience is common among people wanting to change their lives. I began praying earnestly to God, asking for opportunities that would infuse my life with meaning. I confessed my lack of courage to initiate change independently and sought His intervention. I promised to embrace any disruptions with grace and peace, and true to His promise, God answered my prayers. This came to fruition when an external firm acquired a portion of our clientele, triggering a chain of events that led to my layoff.

> "All we have to decide is what to do with
> the time that is given to us."
> – J. R. R. Tolkien

8 DELAYING THE BLESSING

I wish that I could say this is where my Decided journey began. But it wasn't. Despite having spent the last six months yearning for a better life, fear and a lack of savings led me to hastily replace my old life with a very similar one. Within a week I had secured another job, however, in this role I was solely an advisor, liberated from the burdens of operations. It felt like an answer to my prayers. I've come to realize that when you surrender the outcomes of your prayers to God, His solutions may not coincide with your initial expectations. At the time I didn't understand the importance of having a well-defined vision, nevertheless I found renewed purpose and fulfillment in my new role. I became highly productive and acquired new skills and knowledge. Unfortunately, achieving a healthy work-life balanced seemed elusive as I routinely worked twelve hours a day, including weekends.

My new job required travel and for a homebody like me, that was a serious challenge. I did make the best of the experience by exploring local restaurants instead of opting for national chains and immersing myself in the city's art scene. It's worth noting that the people in Minnesota were incredibly kind! A simple three-block walk from my hotel to a restaurant turned into a heartwarming experience, receiving over two dozen greetings and high-fives from the friendly locals. Their kindness alone made the walk in the sweltering heat worthwhile.

In my eagerness to prove myself to my firm, I took on an overwhelming number of tasks. Last minute travel commitments often led to short-notice cancellations of my personal plans. In just a few months my life had transformed from dull to disorderly. The stress of traveling, packing, and unpacking, managing rental cars, irregular meals, inadequate sleep, cancelled dates and demanding work began to take a toll. I spent a lot of time away from home in airports and hotel rooms. However, being part of a team was an absolute delight and I adored and respected my colleagues. Each person possessed an exceptional blend of intelligence, integrity, and unwavering dedication. Not only did they meet the highest standards of our industry, but they also embodied professionalism and kindness. Beyond colleagues, they became friends.

Throughout this period, my house was spotless, and my fridge was empty since I was rarely home. With my son having moved out, I became aware of the emptiness that cast a sullen atmosphere throughout every room. I chose to lift the mood by immersing myself in a steady stream of podcasts and YouTube videos. It dawned on me that, inadvertently, I had accepted life by default.

Without realizing it I was on a quest for something, although I couldn't quite articulate what it was. Every morning and evening I listened to brave souls sharing their stories of struggle and success. I found solace and inspiration in their accounts of leaping and failing and leaping again. Among my favorite orators were Les Brown, Steve Harvey, Mel Robbins, Lisa Nicholes, Joel Osteen, and Trent Shelton. Their voices reminded me that I was capable of more than I had been contributing to the world.

Listening to their words of faith and challenge on a regular basis for nearly a year, I heard their 'I Decided!' moments. Rather than resigning themselves to the status quo and hoping for the best, or simply praying to avoid the worst, they made a firm decision to shift their lives. As I continued to listen to these speeches over the next few months, those words became the treasure I expected to hear in one form or another. I eagerly waited for them with a metaphorical ear highlighter.

During this time, I was helping people work toward their financial goals, but I had neglected my own life goals. It took several months of introspection and ample moments of solitude to realize this oversight. I understood the necessity of a vision for my future, something that was absent. I had simply been surviving. I needed to clarify who I aspired to be and the lifestyle I wanted to live. For years since my divorce, I had been immobilized by fear and desperate for security.

One day I encountered Steve Harvey's compelling story of his journey into comedy. If you haven't heard his account of October 8th I strongly recommend seeking it out and listening to his words. Despite always having a knack for humor and telling jokes throughout his life, Steve had never considered making a living through comedy. An invitation from a friend to a comedy club changed everything. He sat spellbound in the audience as the revelation of a life of comedy revealed itself. He eagerly signed up to appear onstage the following week, however once again fate intervened, and he was called to stage that very night with no time to prepare. Without hesitation he took the stage and captivated the audience. His jokes flowed and he was so entertaining that he won the amateur prize of $50. That victory changed him. He cried all the way home and quit his job the next day to become a full-time comedian. Now that's faith! That was a DECISION!!! Inspired by Steve's story, I decided that when an opportunity presented itself to me, I would embrace it. I would leap! I accepted the fact that I didn't need to have all the answers, nor did I need to know how this change would unfold; I simply needed to trust God, and His wisdom. Recognizing that I was now the person I needed to be in order for an opportunity to arise it wasn't long before the opportunity I had been praying for presented itself and without hesitation I leaped!

And then I cried for three weeks!

As the dust from my leap settled and the reality of my decision set in, an overwhelming flood of emotions engulfed me. I was now in unchartered waters with no oars, no anchor, no wind. I didn't regret my decision, but I hadn't fully analyzed its impact beforehand, nor had I tried to negotiate a better foundation. Shortly after my leap, I realized the full extent of the income I had surrendered, the

401(k) contributions I would never receive, and the responsibility for health insurance benefits that now rested solely on me. My tears were not tears of despair but rather a poignant expression of the profound transformation unfolding within me and the gratitude as I embraced my true purpose. I held steadfast to my conviction that I made the right decision. But it was not easy.

My initial panic was a natural response to the unfamiliar character that had developed in me. I acknowledged the risks involved in pursuing this new direction, as well as my abilities, and embraced the possibilities that would result from my decision. There were moments of reflection and doubt that creeped in from time to time for the next few years, but I reminded myself of the quiet suffering I had endured and reaffirmed the decision of my unfulfilled self.

During one of my most fearful moments, my dear friend Leesa shared invaluable insight with me: "You can't run from fear, but you can run toward God." Her words resonated with me, and each time fear gripped my heart, I turned the fear to faith and handed it back to God. This was not easy at first considering my inclination to handle everything on my own. I was a self-reliant, analytical woman who thrived on charts, graphs, and to-do lists. It took the better part of a year to surrender my fears fully and readily to God. Little did I know I would have to make this same surrender sacrifice several times more over the next few years, however, each time the peace came more quickly, and my faith was stronger.

Discovering the power of gospel music played a significant role in my transformation as it disrupted negative thoughts that taunted me. I wish that I could say that my path was smooth, but that was not the reality. I had moments of victory, and moments of setback. I had dark days where the fear took hold, and I literally didn't want to get out of bed. My remedy was to turn on a podcast or YouTube video and allow a stranger to speak words of faith into me. On one of those dark days, I heard the utterance: "if you're ready to give up, congratulations, you've made it farther than most people." I wish I could remember who said this because that was exactly what I needed to hear in that moment. It was perfect timing. I'm not surprised though - when you make a decision to change your life, God instructs the universe to help you. I decided every day to choose faith over fear. Read that again – I had to choose every single day.

I was resolute in my determination not to look back, yet I couldn't resist casting a slight glimpse over my shoulder at my former life. I contemplated how much simpler my daily existence might be and how my savings could have flourished if I had not taken the leap. I was not prepared for the feelings I would possess, the sentimental longings for predictability. I had healed much in the last couple of years, and it was difficult to recall the lack my heart felt before I made the leap. However, my decision was unwavering - I would no longer neglect my own talents and passions. I would provide value to the world, and in return, I would be rewarded. My story is still being written, with each unfolding chapter presenting its own set of triumphs and challenges to learn from. As I prepare to publish this book I am taking yet a new leap. Deciding my own destiny is not only a privilege; it's my responsibility.

> "Every man got a right to decide his own destiny."
> – Bob Marley

> "Failure is only the end if you decide to stop".
> – Richard Branson

9 UNVEILING THE ART OF CHOICE

Not everyone harbors a desire for change as they are already living their best fabulous life. They find contentment in a good, joyful, exciting, or peaceful existence. However, for those who are not filled with joy and are genuinely prepared to embrace the pursuit of an extraordinary life, there will come a period of restlessness. You make decisions every day and sometimes making no decision is a decision. One way or another, you are making decisions that will exert influence on your life, whether consciously or unconsciously. Embrace the restlessness within you as it is a testament to your readiness to transcend mediocrity.

As you inch closer to the decision to leap, you might

find yourself openly sharing your aspirations with friends and family. As they observe the transformation taking place within you, be prepared for some people to try to dissuade you. While their intentions may be well-meaning, they might undermine your aspirations because they fear that your growth may surpass their own, or that you might outgrow them. Additionally, they may experience a sense of judgment, whether internal or perceived from you if they are content with their life. In my opinion, it is wise to hold your plans and passions close to your heart for a while, unless your decision directly impacts those around you. Preserve the uncluttered purity of the vision. Instead of disclosing your decision to make a change, consider surprising them with the results.

Praying for change is not enough. Wishing for change is not enough. Waiting for change is not enough. Even taking action may not be enough if it stems from a place of desire rather that a committed decision. Prematurely quitting when you don't see any change, or when setbacks occur is a common pitfall. It may seem easy to quit but summoning the courage to relinquish a dream once you've embarked on its pursuit, especially when accountable to others, is challenging. However, before surrendering too hastily, entertain the notion that you might be in a slingshot moment. This analogy was shared by a fellow church member who was describing a difficult time in his life. He suggested that rather than failing, perhaps you're simply experiencing the tension of the slingshot being pulled backward which is necessary in order to propel you forward. It's uncomfortable and frightening, yet an indispensable part of the journey.

On one hand there are those who leap willingly into their decisions, brimming with excitement and enthusiasm. They possess the resources to navigate challenges, including savings, a supportive network of friends and family, and a well-crafted plan. These resources contribute greatly to their favorable outcomes as they wholeheartedly pursue their goals with unwavering determination. As a result, they often achieve remarkable success. On the other hand, some individuals take the leap when they hit rock bottom, recognizing an intrinsic need to rise, take action, and be their own rescue. In their situation, the decision seems almost preordained.

Somewhere in between these extremes are individuals who choose to leap despite lacking enthusiasm. They have hovered near rock bottom, trapped in a perpetual state of monotony, yearning for change but not feeling compelled to take action. In essence, they haven't genuinely decided to change. The problem is that the suspended stagnation appears to be functioning adequately; they're simply unhappy. While both rock bottom and near rock bottom present formidable challenges, it could be argued that those near rock bottom face particularly burdensome circumstances, making it even more difficult than being at rock bottom. While both groups contend with their inner demons, the person who leaps without conviction has not truly decided to change their life. They believe they are willing to leap even if it means potential failure, because the prospect of leaping holds more promise than continuing a dreary and uninspiring existence. The problem is, they lack a vision of the future; they are merely evading the present. As a result, they are likely to encounter failure if they cannot overcome the inevitable obstacles.

Regardless of which scenario a person faces, they share a common reality with so many in the same boat: limited resources and only two options before them – sink or swim! While the idea of allowing yourself to sink might seem tempting as it offers a momentary respite from the struggle, a chance to cease the fight and surrender, it is crucial to remember that you still have a move to make with a pool of possibilities before you. In the words of legend Yogi Berra "It ain't over till it's over". Take a pause from your panic and dive back into the "what-if" arena. Here is where your vision becomes a life preserver until you are able to swim toward shore.

I have been fortunate to be surrounded by incredible, accomplished, and compassionate friends and family, yet there were periods in my life when I felt utterly alone, devoid of options, and without any vision of the future. Since this book has found its way into your life I know that you possess the strength to swim. There is greatness inside of you. Make the decision to swim with unwavering determination, as if you are being pursued by devil sharks - because in a sense you are. Sinking goes against our very nature as human beings. We are created to fight for life but that does not mean you have to do it alone. Remember, God is always with you. Whether or not you have a relationship with Him, He has chosen you. God will not impose Himself on you, so the decision lies with you whether or not you choose to walk with Him.

My heartfelt desire for you is to have a source of solace and comfort during moments of confusion. Even if you are alone, remember that empathy can often be found in the kindness of strangers. You don't have to possess all of the answers in this instant. There is no need for an exhaustive checklist to correct every flaw and amend every mistake. Your sole task in this moment is to decide that you want a better life, and the next right move will reveal itself to you.

These words also apply to the second category of leapers. To those stuck in a perpetual state of mundaneness, my heart goes out to you! Making the decision to leap is particularly challenging for this group. You might be the ones to harbor the most profound regrets if your decision does not turn out the way you envision. Your life right now is tolerable, not horrible, but not exceptional either. Your struggle may not be evident because your days bring a certain level of contentment, especially in a job where you are likely competent. When asked how you're doing, your response is a simple "fine". FINE. This four-letter word has sabotaged many dreams. F.I.N.E. allows people to merely survive day after day, week after week, year after year. It's not an inherently negative word, but it becomes one when your soul yearns for liberation. In my view, 'fine' translates to Functional Indifferent Numbed Existence. The truth is that feeling fine rarely compels change. It lulls us into a false belief that there will always be time to pursue our desires and that now is not that time.

Those who settle for being 'fine' often have income sufficient to pay their bills and occasionally indulge in some of their modest wants. However, they must choose their wants wisely, because selecting one means delaying another. Saving money for a year or two may allow them to enjoy one of these desires, perhaps a week in paradise, but that is not much of a life. If the goal is to escape the life they live each day, then a week in paradise must be savored, like the sprinkles on a doughnut, knowing it will end, and the mundane life will return. I have been in this situation, trying to imprint the view from my hotel balcony or the thrill of the theme park ride into my memory. I have captured photos of every moment of the day, focusing on documenting the experience to recall at a later date rather than fully immersing myself in the meal or entertainment happening right in front of me. After all, these are simply fleeting moments in an otherwise monotonous life. Once back at home, the boredom settles back in.

I've noticed that people who genuinely enjoy life are often too engrossed in the present moment to capture and share every single detail. They capture spontaneous photos here and there, and on rare occasion stage specific shots. They live in the present moment. However, I've also encountered individuals who manufacture moments solely for the purpose of sharing them on social media. They visit places, attend events, and have wardrobe changes just to create the perfect post. In the process, they disrupt precious moments in order to capture the memory of a life they're not fully present for. As they lower the camera, the fake smiles fade, the kids beg to leave, and the spouse vies for attention. These people lie awake at night strategizing and plotting their next fake life moments while their genuine life slips away.

Do you find yourself settling for 'fine', sensing that something is missing despite efforts to fill those gaps - seeking a better job, committing to a new relationship, or buying a larger house? Yet the anticipated joy remains elusive. Here we are, living in the mundane fineness of a decent life. As mentioned before, the decision to leap is particularly daunting for people in this group because there is nothing wrong. Why risk making life worse by taking an unnecessary leap? It's a question worth pondering. You can choose to remain where you are, embracing this decent existence, earning a paycheck while yearning for the weekend, praying away five days of your life. Perhaps you attend a mid-week concert, a brief respite in this average life. If happiness fades as soon as the movie ends, the food is consumed, or your lover leaves your bed, it's clear that a change is needed. Trying to convince yourself that you're happy when deep down you lack true joy won't work. Gratitude is a great way to shift your life in a positive direction but listing things you are grateful for every morning is not going to create serious change. Change requires action, and actions results from a decision. When you genuinely live a joyful life, your joy remains constant regardless of external circumstances.

So, I ask you again, are you really FINE?

Have you ever wondered why wealthy individuals keep working, pondering that if you had their money you'd retire and live on a beach, or indulge in some other leisurely fantasy? If that's you, then you might not be truly living your purpose. When you derive joy from your work, even amid problems and obligations, you don't spend your days wishing for change. Living a purposeful life is one of the keys in attaining true joy and dispelling any dark void of emptiness. Your purpose doesn't need to be something grand, like saving the manatees, but rather it can be something beautifully simple. The key is to identify something that you, in your unique way, can contribute to this world. What matters is that you consciously decide to make the contribution, and then actively follow through on that decision with purposeful action.

The essence of a DECIDED varies for each person, encompassing both profound life transformations and smaller yet impactful choices. It might involve leaving your job to start your own business, closing your business to reenter the workforce, adopting a nomadic lifestyle fueled by online income, ending a toxic relationship, decluttering your living space, or making a radical change to your physical appearance. Your DECIDED is deeply personal to you and holds profound significance in your life. Allowing someone else to decide for you results in a loss for both parties. True change only occurs when you personally make the decision. Otherwise, you are merely going through the motions, and such motions are unlikely to endure. The nature of your leap is shaped by your circumstances and the decision is exclusively yours. You can either dwell on your problems or decide to change them.

> "I decided to see every problem as the opportunity to find a solution."
> – Walt Disney

10 MAKING EFFECTIVE DECISIONS

Since you're still reading, it's likely that you're contemplating a significant change in your life so I'm here to offer guidance navigating the leap with greater ease and minimizing potential hardships.

A crucial first step before taking the leap, if possible, is to prioritize saving as much money as you can. The specific amount varies for each individual, but having a financial cushion provides increased flexibility and resilience. It's noteworthy that the absence of substantial funds can motivate some people to hustle and grind, pushing them to work harder and step out of their comfort zones. An empty bank account may be just the incentive you need to make that cold call. However, for other individuals the lack of financial security might discourage them and lead to premature resignation. I tend to fall into the second category, whereby I am physically immobilized when funds are short. Understanding your relationship with money is crucial. Assess your comfort level and determine the amount of savings that will provide you with a reasonable safety net. Remember, everyone's path is unique, and the challenges encountered contribute to personal growth. Thoughtful financial preparation can alleviate stress associated with the decision, enabling you to courageously pursue your goals.

Second, write down your best-case scenario and end goal. While your vision may evolve over time, it's essential to have a clear target to focus on. While I hope your journey is smooth, it's essential to acknowledge that the future may be filled with highs and lows. In preparation for the challenging moments, write a heartfelt letter to your future self. Capture your current thoughts, emotions, and the reasons behind your decision for change. Clarify your 'WHY' – the driving force that will sustain you through challenges and doubts. Months into your new endeavor, or out of that relationship, or whatever moments of defeat and sadness you are facing, you might be tempted to romanticize the past and question your choices. Revisiting the words penned by your past self serves as a powerful reminder of the emptiness, grief, lack of appreciation you experienced as well as the exhilaration that marked the beginning of your 'Decided' journey. Even though time may have distanced you from those feelings, trust the 'you' that wrote those words and honor them.

Within your letter, include words of encouragement – a congratulatory letter to your future self. Let your future self know how immensely proud you are for persevering through the challenging moments. Remind yourself that you are worthy of this victory, and the world stands to benefit from the work you are undertaking, no matter how big or small your decision. These encouraging words will allow you to connect with your past self, providing solace and inspiration during times of doubt and reaffirming your commitment to your journey. Believe in your abilities, have confidence in your decisions, and let the words you've written serve as a guiding light through the challenges and triumphs ahead. Your dedication to personal growth and your willingness to pursue a more fulfilling life are testaments to your courage and resilience.

Third, break down your ultimate goal into smaller manageable steps with flexible deadlines. These deadlines, to borrow a phrase from "Pirates of the Caribbean", should act as guidelines, not strict rules, allowing room for adjustments. By dividing your overarching objective into smaller milestones, you maintain a clear sense of direction in your journey. Remember, the purpose of these smaller goals and deadlines is to guide you, not create unnecessary pressure or limitations. Life is filled with unexpected events and your path may not always align with your preferred timeline. Embrace the understanding that these deadlines provide structure, not punishment. If you find yourself deviating from your planned timeline, take a moment to assess the delay and make necessary modifications to your plan. Your ability to adapt and stay resilient will play a crucial role in your ultimate success. Celebrate these milestones along the way and keep track your progress to stay motivated.

Fourth, find your tribe. Building a support system during a transitional phase can be powerful as your tribe will support you and uplift you when you are struggling. Let's be honest, you will encounter struggles. When you surround yourself with individuals who share similar visions or who have already navigated a similar journey, you can lean on them for guidance and encouragement when you need it most. There will be unexpected obstacles, setbacks, delays, and moments when others let you down. It's remarkable how helping someone else overcome their obstacles helps you overcome your own. Some days you'll be the one providing support, and on other days they'll be there for you. Your tribe doesn't necessarily have to be composed of your closest friends; in fact, your closest friends might be your most vocal critics. Rather your tribe could initially include strangers you connect with through networking groups. These tribe members don't even have to belong to your same industry or share identical aspirations. Surprisingly, the advice you receive from someone unfamiliar with your industry can be refreshing and insightful! However even if they are in the same field as you, it's likely that your strengths are different from your competitor's, and you are most likely not competing for the same clients.

Individuals naturally align themselves with people who share their values and experiences. Adopting an abundance mindset reveals that there is ample room for everyone to thrive. Each of us brings a unique approach, a distinct voice, and a target audience that resonates with our authentic selves. Keep in mind that forming your tribe is an ongoing process that might require some time. You don't need to postpone building this tribe until after making your decision to leap. Seek mentors, coaches or groups that align with your vision. Attend workshops, events and conferences that will further your interests. Seize opportunities to connect with others and be intentional about building genuine relationships. What matters most is that the people in your tribe embody an uplifting and forward-thinking mindset. In a world filled with discouragement and excuses, your tribe should be composed of creative thinkers actively seeking solutions.

I have cultivated multiple tribes. My entrepreneurial journey began two months before Covid made its way to the United States. Starting a new business venture with the constraint of in-person meetings, I discovered various online groups that became my lifeline. Despite the isolation of working from home, these strangers quickly transformed into cherished confidants. We established weekly Zoom meetings to support and uplift each other, sharing our triumphs and setbacks. We sought valuable advice and gained profound insights that we would not have achieved on our own. Through consistent virtual meetings, we engaged in discussions about our businesses, and we tapped into a wealth of resources. The collective wisdom and varied perspectives within the group became an endless wellspring of motivation and ideas. In a time of uncertainty and turmoil, these online tribes reassured me that I was not alone in my journey. Our shared experiences within this dedicated community served as a source of encouragement during difficult weeks. We could voice our concerns openly, free from the fear of being perceived as complainers.

Having the ability to articulate our worries to someone who understands that we are not asking for permission to give up, but rather seeking support and understanding, is invaluable. What you need is a cheerleader, not someone who will encourage you to surrender.

Within my tribes, we discovered that our skills frequently complemented each other, creating a collective reservoir of wisdom and an extensive network of contacts to exchange. Whenever possible, we engaged each other's businesses, allowing us to identify weaknesses in our processes without the potentially damaging impact of a bad review. Throughout the turbulent months of the pandemic, our businesses grew through the power of collaboration.

That leads me to the fifth and final point: Clearly define your values. While there is an entire industry devoted to branding your business, the essence lies in understanding your core values and ensuring that your business accurately reflects those values. Many people waste considerable time and effort trying to be the business they think they should be, in order to attract everyone as a customer. Instead, it's crucial to identify your ideal customers and focus on serving them. This way you won't risk expending valuable time and energy attempting to cater to the masses. It's important to recognize that growth and expansion can happen gradually and in a sustainable manner. An example is Amazon which began as a humble bookseller and is now one of the largest retailers and e-commerce businesses in the world. You too can evolve and become a solution for a broader audience over time. Focus first on serving people who share your core values.

The process of launching a business or striving to attain your dreams can, at time, dampen your joy. When you hold a distinct end goal in your mind, but struggle with materializing it, discouragement can seep in. You might find yourself compelled to create more spreadsheets, engage in more networking, or intensify advertising, thinking these efforts will push you forward. While these efforts may work, I also find that taking a moment to pause and ask for guidance from God can be helpful. I believe that God should be included in every part of your life. He wants you to succeed and to be a blessing so that you can, in turn, be a blessing to others.

I vividly remember a week when discouragement weighed heavily on me, and I began to question my commitment toward my goal. While attending church one Sunday Pastor Bekah Craig, provided just the boost I needed. She was speaking on joy, a very simple concept, and she expressed this sentiment so eloquently: "It is a decision to say I am not going to let the enemy steal my joy." Once again, there was that word: decision. It was in that moment that I learned the importance of actively guarding my joy and paying close attention to the lessons God was imparting. This decision must be reaffirmed each day. The enemy will tirelessly work to steal your joy, especially when it senses your potential for success. The greater your potential, the greater your opposition. It shouldn't come as a surprise if challenges begin to emerge within your home, among your loved ones or even in the form of persistent issues like a vehicle or appliance breaking down. The enemy does not want you to succeed, and he will employ every tactic to make you quit. By consciously choosing joy despite the obstacles, you are not only preserving your own well-being but also affirming your determination to triumph over adversity. Remember, the enemy's tactics are aimed at distracting you from your path and undermining your resolve.

While these steps above may appear to be strictly business-oriented, they are equally applicable to personal matters. At the heart of each is identifying your core beliefs, clarifying what you inherently deserve, and discerning who you want to be.

Late in life I took up the violin, and many in my circle wondered if my newfound interest was sparked by Lindsey

I DECIDED

Stirling. Unaware of who she was at first, I grew curious and decided to explore her story. Her narrative is a remarkable testament to choosing one's identity. She decided who she wanted to be – a dancing violinist - and made a resolute decision about fearlessly pursuing the life she envisioned. She dedicated herself to mastering her arts, captivating audiences through the fusion of violin music and dance. She cultivated a performance featuring imaginative costumes and choreography that enchanted spectators of all ages. Her journey and decision to embrace self-love resonated profoundly with me.

> "The same way that I practiced the violin, the same way that I practiced my dance moves, I decided that I was going to practice being positive and practice loving myself."
>
> - Lindsey Stirling

11 PRAY FOR COURAGE, NOT A RESCUE

I wish to recognize that not every DECIDED is filled with a positive outcome, fueled by joy. Certain decisions carry with them a weight of sadness and regret, even when made in the best interest of ourselves or others at the time. Despite understanding the necessity of these decisions, doubt, sorrow, and guilt may persist. We are not immune to these emotions simply because our rational mind is convinced it was the right thing to do.

The decision to euthanize a beloved pet often comes with doubt as well as sorrow. Doubt about the necessity and timing, accompanied by a potential sense of shame if financial considerations were a determining factor. I've known individuals who, due to financial constraints, could not afford surgery for an injured pet, leaving euthanasia as the only option to prevent prolonged suffering. It's an agonizing decision that can persist without end. Choosing the right time is equally distressing. Is today the day, or should it be Monday, after one last weekend together? Doubt inevitably creeps in, and time, is a liar. One moment, our pet appears fine, and the next, an incident compels us to admit, 'it's time'. Even if there is no doubt about the necessity of the action, the decision transforms into grief as you acknowledge that your beloved pet, who cannot offer consent, is at your mercy. In the span of a single year, I faced this decision twice. The first time, the decision was unclear in its timing and brought with it incredible doubt and tears; the second time, it was abundantly clear that I was making the correct and compassionate choice.

The decision to leave a spouse when the relationship has broken down, therapy has failed to bridge the divide, and the parties' goals and values are no longer aligned seems an obvious and simple decision to anyone outside of the marriage. However, the reality is far from simple. It's crucial not to let anyone diminish the complexity of the situation and the gravity of the decision. You've shared intimate moments with your spouse that no one else has experienced. You've made vows to this person that no one else has made. The decision to leave or stay belongs to each of you. Though recognizing the potential impact your decision may have on those around you is crucial, it's essential to acknowledge that others won't be held accountable for your choice. Thoughtfully consider the repercussions of your decision. Leaving is a decision you make once, while staying is a decision reaffirmed every day.

But what about the decision to part ways with a spouse when nothing seems obviously wrong? There are no conflicts, just a cordial coexistence. A blasé companionship based on similar interests and goals. Yet, there is a subtle sense of something missing, a yearning for a deeper or more passionate connection. It feels selfish to dissolve the marriage in pursuit of a potentially happier and more fulfilling relationship, but it also seems foolish to stay simply for the sake of keeping a promise made in younger years. How do you navigate this decision? I appreciate Billy Graham's perspective on this; he suggests praying for renewed passion for your spouse and seeking ways to move beyond the perceived boredom. (BillyGraham.org). Perhaps one spouse is content with the status quo even though you both now resemble roommates rather than loving partners. I think decisions of this nature are the most difficult to make because you are opting for a course of action that is lacking a true catalyst.

Another difficult decision arises when the necessity to move your parent to a care facility becomes imperative due to urgent medical requirements. Despite the emotional and financial considerations that may accompany this decision, when it aligns with the best interest of your parent, the choice becomes evident. Navigating this decision becomes notably challenging when medical needs are not a primary concern, and you have the space to accommodate them in your home. In such cases, the considerations extend to include other individuals, such as a spouse, or children, making it crucial to acknowledge and validate the feelings of everyone involved. The complexity intensifies when conflicting desires among those affected come into play.

Decided of this nature carry substantial emotional weight, encompassing both pain and sorrow, but can also evoke profound appreciation and love. It's crucial to navigate this decision with a comprehensive understanding of specific care needs, the availability of support systems, and the impact on your family dynamics.

What if there a person in your life who treats you as if you are the same person you were in high school despite the fact that you graduated thirty years ago? Some people never allow you to grow past your mistakes. Even in adulthood, some might perceive you only as they did in childhood. If you allow them to, they will keep you in that state forever, held to the decisions you made and the actions you took in your youth. They attempt to confine you to a mold of who they believed you were, mentally trapping you in your previous embodiment, which is rarely an accurate portrayal to begin with. By overlooking the changes you've undergone as a result of the multitude of your decisions since then, they do not have to acknowledge the person you have become. This often manifests with them projecting an image of you to everyone around you, anchored in outdated perceptions rather than embracing who you are today. Those individuals were not present for every decision of your life, yet they hold you immobilized in their mind, disregarding your individual journey. They persist in portraying you as the same person you were as a child, as their spouse or as their coworker. In this case, do you keep this person in your life trying to convince them that you have changed? Or do you decide to remove them as best you can?

In the midst of these heart-wrenching decisions, you may decide to seek professional guidance. I strongly believe in seeking the advice and opinions of others, so long as you do not surrender your sovereignty to them. Regardless of the influences that guide you to your chosen journey, what holds genuine significance is the bravery and resolve to live an authentic life, resisting external influence that seek to define your identity. Make a decision each day that actively contributes to shaping you into the person you aspire to be. Identify the life you want with such clarity that you reject any counterfeit version of yourself and possess the strength to resist temptation to surrender.

It is going to be hard. There will be suffering. Yet, entrust your concerns to God, seek courage and strength through prayer, rather than pleading for a rescue.

> "God does not build champions by removing adversity. He gives them courage. Pray for Courage."
>
> – Pastor Colin Higginbottom

12 PRACTICAL DECISION-MAKING STRATEGIES

1. DECIDE to keep your word.

The simplest way to keep your word is to refrain from saying yes when you truly mean no.

I grew frustrated with commitments I reluctantly made to people, commitments I didn't genuinely want. Despite my desire to say no, I said yes out of a sense of guilt, since I had the time and resources. I wasn't seeking approval; rather saying "no" seemed selfish. Soon my days and nights were full of obligations to others, and after years of dedicating my time and energy to causes and people that didn't align with my true values left me feeling bitter. One day I woke with a feeling of dread over the obligations I had for that week. I knew a change was necessary, so I decided to never again say yes when my thoughts, heart and soul were screaming "no". That day I created my YES/NO checklist shown below. There are situations in which I say 'yes' to a request and later wish that I had declined. In these situations, I keep my word and fulfill the obligation with care and enthusiasm. However, now when asked to volunteer, I kindly request 24 hours to respond. If not granted, my answer is an automatic "no". If given the time to reflect, I consult my checklist and identify what I must sacrifice in order to say yes to this request, as every decision comes with an opportunity cost.

When I first created the checklist I frequently referred to it in the weeks that followed, and the ease to which the 'no' came after honest consideration was surprising. Reflecting on the countless 'yeses' I had avoided brought me to tears. I realized how many hours I had been giving away just to avoid feeling selfish. Now I devote my time and resources to people and causes that align with my heart.

1. *Is this opportunity in alignment with my purpose?*
2. *Am I willing to set aside my personal goals to devote time or resources to this endeavor?*
3. *Will I honor this commitment by devoting the time required?*
4. *Is my answer a resounding yes?*
5. *Am I reluctant to say no for any reason, and if so, what is that reason?*

I have goals that I desire to achieve, and my time is scarce. I acknowledge that this request or opportunity is a valid and worthy one, and particularly important to the person asking me. But saying 'yes' to this opportunity means saying 'no' to something that I have already determined is valuable to me. If I am hesitant to say 'yes', then I must say 'no' without hesitation in order to honor myself.

2. DECIDE every day to improve your situation, no matter how small.

I composed this book in small increments of about 10 to 15 minutes a day over several months as anything more would have seemed too daunting. The accumulation of small efforts, added here and there, resulted in the completion of this book. It began as a vision and materialized one paragraph at a time. If you're striving toward a goal, consider taking a daily action step, whether big or small. This approach, known as the Swiss cheese method, involves utilizing the small openings in your day to complete a task.

3. DECIDE to find the treasure.

I learned there is treasure in every encounter, obstacle, sorrow, and person. Although it may not be obvious initially, there is something valuable that you can glean and apply to your life, moving you in a positive direction. Even if the subject of a discussion doesn't particularly interest you, or the interaction is an overall negative one, recognize that there is a gem waiting to be found, and then listen attentively for it. This will help you focus positively and is a productive use of your time. Every sorrowful situation can teach you more about yourself and help you to identify what truly matters to you. Most importantly, decide to find the treasure in people. The value you give to people is your attention and the value you give to your self is to listen.

4. DECIDE to speak up.

Many people express difficulty in speaking up for themselves. Personally, I've never had that problem, perhaps because I have never had an advocate to speak on my behalf. If you've struggled to assert yourself verbally, understand that you don't need anyone's permission. You don't have to share every opinion, but when confronted by a situation that diminishes you, I encourage you to speak up. Approach the person with respect, and assertively communicate your thoughts and needs to ensure your perspective is acknowledged. Like many aspects of life, improvement comes with practice. Looks for small opportunities to practice and be mindful not to fixate on the negatives around you.

5. DECIDE You Are Worth It

You are worth it. You are a beautiful soul and God created you to live an abundant life. Living in lack, poverty, or struggle is a righteous misconception. Living a life of 'just enough' reflects a self-centered existence, rooted in selfishness, stemming from various factors such as insecurity, fear, or lack of empathy. The Marriam-Webster dictionary defines selfish as: concerned excessively or exclusively with oneself: seeking or concentrating on one's own advantage, pleasure, or well-being without regard for others. To avoid selfishness, it's crucial to act with regard for others and embrace the truth that you are meant for abundance. I believe it is necessary to work to be as successful as your talents and intellect allow, so you can be a blessing to others. You can be generous with your money, time, attention, or talents. At its core, generosity begins with a decision to extend beyond your own needs through tangible gestures of kindness, words of encouragement, or even through prayer for another person. It commences by affirming your worthiness to experience abundance.

6. DECIDE to nourish healthy relationships.

Nourish relationships that bring you peace, joy, and love. Release the expectation of others to treat you well or remain in your life. If someone consistently undermines or belittles you, their negativity might amplify as you make positive changes. Ignore their chatter and let your actions demonstrate your worth and stop trying to convince them of your worthiness. As you work toward your dream life, individuals who resonate with your values and aspirations for a brighter future will naturally gravitate toward you, offering their support, love, and encouragement.

> "I have decided to stick with love. Hate is too great a burden to bear."
> – Martin Luther King, Jr.

13 THE POWER OF SMALL DECISIONS

When my son was 13, he wrote a note to himself declaring that one day he would hold a senior compliance position at Goldman Sachs. Nearly ten years later, he found that note and marveled at how predictive his younger self was, as he did, in fact, become employed as a Senior Compliance Analyst at Goldman Sachs. As I write this book he is the Legal Counsel at a firm that helps businesses and individuals achieve their aspirations of success, health, and financial security. If you told him at the age of 13 that he would earn an undergraduate degree by age 20, graduate Summa Cum Laude, be voted President of Alpha Chi, be voted President of Omicron Delta Epsilon, earn a law degree by age 23, earn his black belt in kenpo karate, become a Division II lacrosse champion, become lead guitarist in a law school band, a Silver Key award winner in art, and a multiple Cali Award winner, he would have been overwhelmed. But he did all of those things, as well as obtain the job of his dreams working in the financial services industry. Most importantly, he married his true love, and became a father to their children. How did he accomplish all this? He made a decision every day to do the little things right.

I'm including in this book the essay my son wrote for his law school application. He wrote this from his heart, and if you've ever read these types of essays, you'll know that he violated many of the so-called 'rules' for essays. Rather than an anecdotal snapshot intended to give a glimpse of who he is by highlighting a single act of kindness or filling the pages with humor and creativity – he flat out told the committee who he is and who he is going to be. Apparently, it was well-received, leading to acceptances from 16 law schools. Ultimately, he chose and attended his top-pick school.

Nathan D. Holtman, Law School Admissions Essay
I hung my Black Belt Certificate on the wall in my room opposite my bed. Every day, this certificate is the first thing I see when I wake up. The significance of this

achievement is more than just a formal recognition of my mastery of American Kenpo Karate; this certificate represents an acceptance to a larger community of black belts who are dedicated to upholding the principles of our dojo: Modesty, Courtesy, Integrity, Self-Control, Perseverance, and Indomitable Spirit. The signatures at the bottom represent the men and women who taught me, encouraged me, and stood by me. I could not have achieved this goal without them.

Before the sparring section of my black belt exam, in the eighth hour, I sat in the changing room, my limbs and body shaking from blood sugar deficiency. I frantically tried to focus my thoughts and energies to recall all that I had learned in the last 15 years. I had several three-on-one fights with other black belts next, and I was nervous. This portion would be tough, and painful, and I remember the feeling that my body was betraying me. Recalling the words of my instructor, I made the conscious effort to execute every single strike, block, and stance with precision and focused perfection. I pressed through the immense pain and muscle spasms and earned my Black Belt. Reflecting upon this achievement, I began seeing parallels elsewhere in my life.

I keep my lacrosse state championship medal on my

top bookshelf. During my senior year in high school, my coach began using the phrase "do the little things right." At first, I was unclear on the significance of the phrase; but slowly, I began seeing its relevance. Executing every little movement, picking up every ground ball, making every pass and shot intentional and focused, was the best way to add value to the team. If we all performed the best we could and recognized that each game was a process, we would always walk away proud of our performance. On the day of our final game, my coach asked me to play the Attack position, rather than my usual position. I thought of his words about the little things, and throughout the game I focused on doing what Attackmen do. That day, I was the leading scorer for our team, and we won the State Game. As a team, we did the little things right.

I hung my "Food & Beverage Staff" lanyard from the Web.com Pro Golf Tour on my bedroom door. I worked two summers as a fry cook in the snack bar at a Country Club. During the Pro Golf Tour, my manager told me to expect the ticket holder above the grill to fill up all the way across the back wall. The words he chose to empower me to remain focused and confident were: "just chip away at it." We knew we could eventually fill every order, and, by "chipping away at it", we did.

I display my "Thank You" card from Utah Legal Services on my nightstand. This card, signed so lovingly from all the staff in the Benefits department, reminds me of the volunteer hours I worked. Prior to this experience, I was never very comfortable speaking to strangers over the phone. However, this position allowed me to practice engaging with others to build relationships. I overcame my initial intimidation by reminding myself to do the little things right, and I chipped away at my case load.

I hung my honorary certificates next to my closet. I reflect upon my academic experiences that lead to my inductions, as well as the dedication of my professors. While I am proud of the recognition, I am humbled by the gratitude I received from two classmates I tutored, both of whom are veterans. To explain difficult mathematical concepts, I applied the doctrines of "doing the little things right" and "chipping away at it", moving through mathematical analysis, sequentially building off of previous steps. They learned quickly to take large, intimidating concepts and break them down into manageable steps.

I keep my vision board leaning against the wall in my room. This board is a visual display of everything I hope to accomplish throughout my life. It allows me to see myself as a successful lawyer, loving husband, and grateful father. I realize these goals are readily attainable if I "do the little things right" and "chip away" at the steps in between. My attendance at law school is the next step in the process. When I am a lawyer, I will create value for my community and for the professional legal sphere through the practice of law. I will employ the black belt principles of my dojo by working with honesty and integrity for the benefit of society. When I am a husband and a father, I will see the continuation of a legacy of excellence.

My vision board is the last thing I see before I go to bed each night. One day, I will get to hang it on the wall and say: "I did the little things right."

As I reread his words for inclusion in this book, I was brought to tears. I watched him as he worked every day to do his very best. He was busy building a life, and it was not easy, nor was the path always clear. The thing about my son is that he never wanted to conquer the world. He never sought fame or fortune. He simply respected himself enough to do his very best to create a life he wanted to live. He seeks peace and joy. People gravitate toward him as he exudes a feeling of harmony and love. I believe because of

I DECIDED

his loving demeanor that these accomplishments came to him gracefully through action. Today, he is a successful lawyer, working at this dream job – the one he described on his vision board when he was 13 years old! He is a father and loving husband, just as he predicted. Just as he decided he would be.

What are you living with right now that you know must change?

How much longer are you going to wait?

The choice is yours.

YOU DECIDE

ABOUT THE AUTHOR

Kelly Holtman is an accomplished artist and financial services professional whose debut book, *I Decided*, is a compelling exploration of her transformative journey. Living in the vibrant intersection of art and finance, Kelly has always found inspiration in the convergence of creativity and strategic thinking.

Kelly brings a unique perspective to her writing, seamlessly blending her analytical mindset with a passion for artistic expression. She leverages her analytical acumen to navigate the complexities of the financial markets while in her personal life dedicating her time passionately advocating for the arts.

I Decided chronicles her personal odyssey, revealing how the power of decision-making became the catalyst for profound change in her life. Her ability to navigate the intricacies of both the financial world and the realm of artistic expression gives her writing a distinctive edge. Her prose is not only insightful but also possesses a unique blend of practical wisdom and imaginative flair.

www.ingramcontent.com/pod-product-compliance
Lightning Source LLC
Chambersburg PA
CBHW060333050426
42449CB00011B/2743